THE
DANISH
ART OF
WHITTLING
SNITTE

THE
DANISH
ART OF
WHITTLING
SNITTE

• • • • • • • •

make beautiful wooden birds

FRANK EGHOLM

BATSFORD

First published in the United Kingdom in 2017 by
Batsford
43 Great Ormond Street
London
WC1N 3HZ

An imprint of Pavilion Books Company Ltd

ISBN 978-1-84994-440-3

A CIP catalogue record for this book is available from the British Library.

10 9 8 7 6 5 4 3 2 1

Reproduction by Mission Productions Ltd, Hong Kong
Printed and bound by Toppan Leefung Printing Ltd, China

This book can be ordered direct from the publisher at www.pavilionbooks.com

CONTENTS

GETTING STARTED

Before you get started on whittling your birds,
make sure all your equipment is in place. On
the following few pages we'll explain how to
design and draw your bird template.

WHITTLING SMALL BIRDS

Small birds with folded wings make really good whittling projects. Adults and children from about the age of 11 can carve birds.

Of course, your first attempt at whittling a bird will be challenging, but it will be easier the second time and practice makes perfect, as the saying goes. Using dry limewood as a material and cutting the bird's outline out of a block of wood first makes the process relatively simple. Lime is a soft wood and easy to carve, but you can also use other soft woods, such as poplar, alder or basswood. The bird can then be mounted in a decorative fashion – for example on a piece of driftwood – and painted.

So, once you are equipped with a sharp knife and a pre-cut block, it's time to whittle.

DRAWING

For templates, see pages 120–123, but you can also find inspiration in bird books and on the Internet.

Use a block of wood with a thickness of about 3.5–4.5cm (1²⁄₅–1⁴⁄₅in).

The simplest method is to draw the profile of a bird on the block of wood, so that the neck and tail are pointing in the same direction along its length. Position the template so that it lies along the wood grain, as otherwise the beak can break easily.

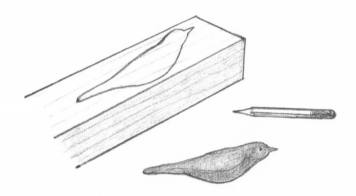

CUTTING OUT THE BIRD SHAPE

Once you're happy with your bird shape, you can start to cut it out. There are several ways you can do this, depending on what equipment you have.

 To cut out the bird shape you can use a scroll saw with a strong blade, or a jigsaw with a narrow blade for curves.

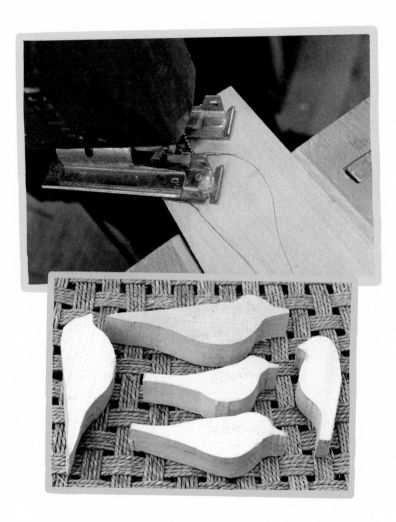

You can also use a fretsaw/hand scroll saw if
you prefer, or a band saw with a narrow blade.

SAFETY

If you are not confident, protect the hand holding the piece of wood with cut-resistant safety Kevlar gloves, for example. See supplier list, page 126. You can also protect your thumb and fingers with leather finger guards (or you can cut the finger off a thick glove).

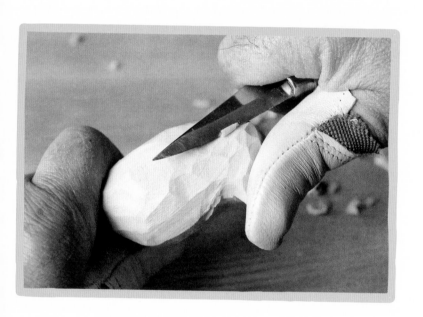

WHITTLING YOUR BIRD

Now it's time to start whittling and bring
your bird to life! There are several different
whittling techniques you can use to make your
bird, all described in this section. If you want
to see videos of techniques and birds being
whittled, go to www.snittesiden.dk.

ROUGH CUTTING

Hold the wood in one hand and cut away from you.
Watch out for your legs!

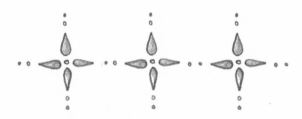

'SCISSOR' TECHNIQUE

Brace your hands against your body, holding the knife in the usual way. Push the knife away from you, and pull the wood back at the same time. You can also twist the knife as you cut.

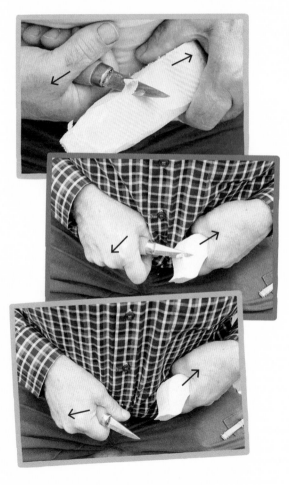

USING A SUPPORT

For extra cutting power, use a tree stump or a block of wood as a support, stand up and cut downwards towards the block. You may also need some support when cutting the back of the bird's neck, as there is not much to hold on to.

USING A
WHITTLING BOARD

Use a whittling board to support the wood when you're sitting down. It is used in the same way as you would when supporting the work on a tree stump or block of wood. See page 124 for instructions for how to make one.

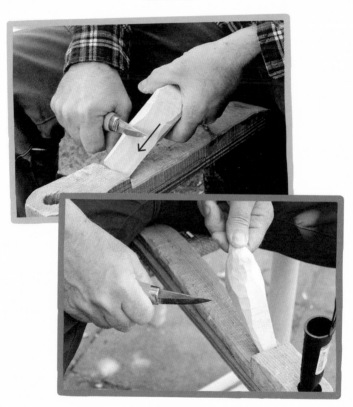

THUMB TECHNIQUE

Your thumb may become sore, so protect it with
a thumb guard if necessary.

Press against the back of the blade. There are three
techniques and these can also be combined.

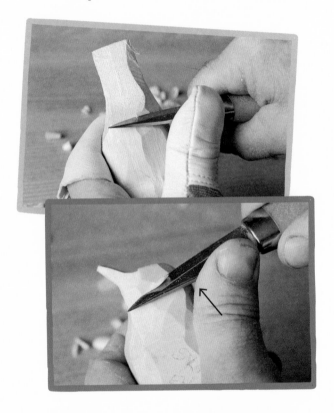

1. Push the knife from behind with your thumb.

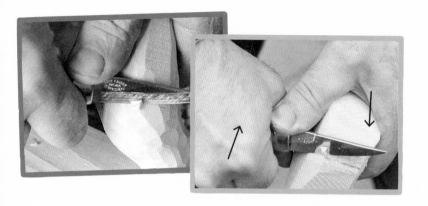

2. Tilt the hand holding the knife backwards, so the blade is tilted forwards.

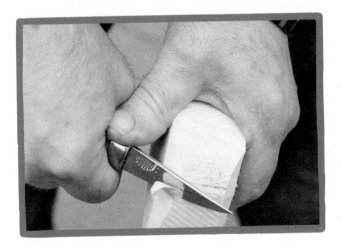

3. Twist the hand holding the knife, so the blade digs into the wood.

PARING
(CUTTING TOWARDS YOU)

Cutting towards your body is a good technique for the neck (and other places) but it is more dangerous and requires practice. If necessary, wear cut-resistant safety gloves. Try to move the knife without digging it downwards into the wood; if it looks like the knife is heading towards your hand, try holding the bird in a different way.

The thumb of the hand holding the knife is braced against the wood while you make small cuts, twisting, tilting or pushing the knife with your fingers. Bracing your thumb against the wood enables you to control the movements of the knife, so there is less risk of it cutting the hand holding the wood.

THE BASIC
BIRD SHAPE

Read through all the instructions carefully before
you begin, then start by smoothing the edges of
the bird to give it a little shape and to make it
comfortable to hold. Use photos and illustrations to
help establish the shape.

DIRECTION OF CUTTING

NB For the neck, see cutting technique on page 24. Smooth off the edges gradually, concentrating on the body, neck and head.

Cut inwards at the head and tail (see diagram below). See cutting technique on page 22 for the beak and on page 38 for the tail.

FINAL CHECK

Is the shape right? Have the sharp edges been pared away?
Is it symmetrical and is the carving even and regular? Should
the head be smaller? Hold the bird in your hand. Does it feel
round and comfortable to hold?

ADDING DETAIL

Birds have many different shapes. They may be round and plump or delicate and slender. The tail may be long or short and there may be a notch in the end (see page 39).

For wing markings and wingtips, see pages 36–37.

Birds do not naturally have a visible neckline but
many people like to mark the neck by carving it,
as above.

BEAKS

Use the point of the knife and thumb technique (see page 22). If the beak crosses the grain of the wood, cut towards you, using protection for your fingers if necessary.

The beak can also be carved separately and
glued into place in a drilled hole.

WINGS

The wings can be marked using V-shaped cuts placed below them to make a gentle curve in relief. Press your thumb against the back of the blade and tilt the knife a little to dig it in. The V-shaped cut can be made more pronounced if you cut from both sides.

WINGTIPS

Carving the wingtips and marking the wings
on the back of the bird is more difficult and
demanding. It is a trickier area to work in and you
are normally cutting against the grain of the wood.

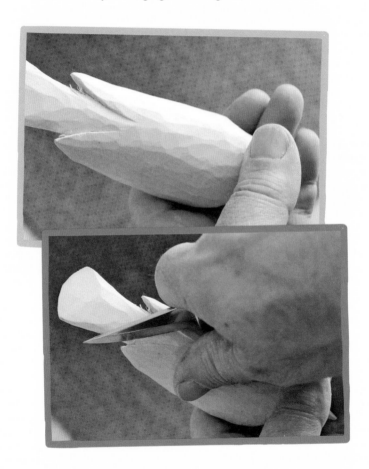

TAILS

There are various ways of carving the tail.
Make small notches in the tail by cutting inwards
from the edges diagonally.

TAIL NOTCHES

Hold your thumb against the side of the tail and cut carefully, using the fingers of your knife hand.

EYES

Use small beads 3–4mm (⅛– ⅙in) in diameter.

1. Mark where the eyes are to go in pencil and then make a tiny indentation using an awl. Take care to ensure that the indentations are positioned symmetrically on either side of the head.

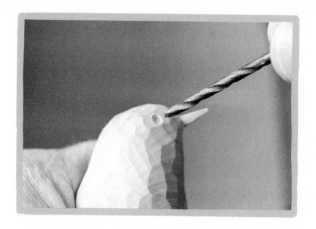

2. Drill holes to fit the diameter of the beads. Drill carefully, turning the drill bit with your fingers. The holes should be two-thirds of the depth of the beads.

3. Glue the beads in place, turning them around so that any holes in the beads are not on show.

EXPRESSIONS

The expression on your bird's face can be true to
life or more naïve – both are equally charming.
The excellent pieces shown here were carved by
12-year-old children.

PAINTING BIRDS

To really bring your birds to life, you can paint them: you can be true to nature or use your own fantastical colours.

GENERAL
PAINTING TIPS

Use acrylic or oil paints. The birds in this book were painted with slightly thinned-down paint, but of course you can also give them a thicker coating if you wish. If you are not used to painting, practise on a piece of plywood or cartridge paper before painting your beautifully carved bird. It can be helpful to use illustrations rather than photographs as a reference, as these tend to show plumage and colour more clearly.

There are various ways of painting, but the main rule is to paint the light colours first. See pages 50–61 for step-by-step instructions.

PAINTING A BULLFINCH

MATERIALS
Carved bird
Illustration
Acrylic paint
Paintbrush

1. Paint the white areas on the wings.

2. Add white on the underside of the bird.

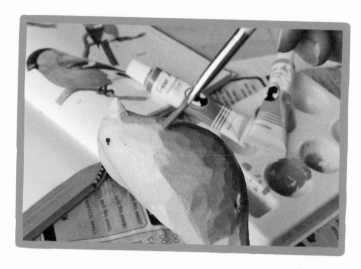

3. Use a thinned-down reddish colour (red and light brown) on the breast.

4. Paint the back of the neck with light grey.

5. Paint in the black areas on the wings, tail and head.

6. Add a greyish beak.

7. If you like, paint thin white streaks on the wings.

PAINTING A BLUE TIT

MATERIALS
Carved bird
Illustration
Acrylic paints
Paintbrush

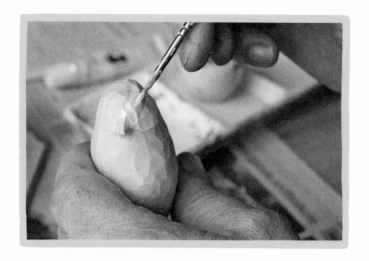

1. Paint the white areas on the head.

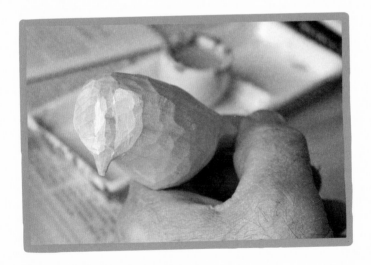

2. Mix a pale blue colour and paint the top of the head.

3. Mix a yellow and paint the breast.

4. Paint the back of the neck green, perhaps mixing a little diluted black into the green.

5. Paint the wings and tail blue, perhaps adding a little very diluted black.

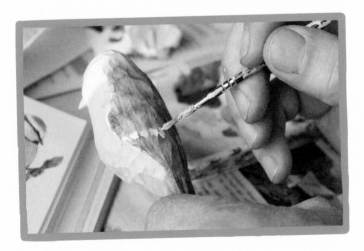

6. Paint white on the back of the head and white markings on the wings.

7. Paint the black markings with small
brush strokes.

DISPLAYING YOUR BIRDS

• • • • • • • • •

A pretty mount can add to the overall
decorative look of the bird. Driftwood from the
beach or fallen branches, twigs and bark from
the forest all make good mounts – there are
some lovely ideas on the following pages.

LEGS

Before inserting the legs, decide what the bird is to be mounted on and in what kind of pose. Here are some interesting ideas to start you off.

1. Make a pair of legs from bamboo skewers or wire, possibly twisted for extra strength. Trim to the right length.

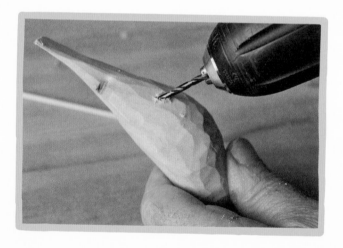

2. Drill two holes in the underside of the bird near the tail. The legs usually point forwards diagonally.

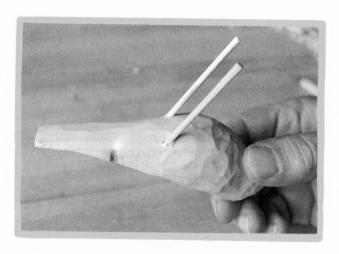

3. Glue the legs in place.

4. Drill holes for the legs in the mount. Note the angle at which you need to drill, depending on whether the bird is to look up, down or straight ahead.

MOUNTING WITHOUT LEGS

To mount without legs, drill a hole in the underside of the bird at an appropriate angle, depending on whether the bird is to look up, down or straight ahead. Glue a length of dowel in the hole, then drill a hole in the mount and glue the dowel into the mount.

If you want to be able to change the direction the bird is facing, insert the dowel without glue.

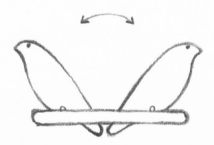

BIRD ON A STICK

To display a bird on a stick, cut an appropriately sized disc from a branch and drill a hole in the centre and in the underside of the bird. Assemble the parts using a piece of metal, twig or dowel. Glue in position if required.

BIRD ON A NEST

Weave a nest from fresh birch twigs to fit your
bird. This can be as neat or as messy as you like.
Then drill a hole in the underside of the bird.
Cut an appropriately sized disc from a branch and
drill a hole through the centre. Countersink the
hole on one side of the disc.

Screw the bird to the disc so that the nest is
held in place in between.

BIRDS ON SMALL TRUNKS

Carved birds look great mounted on small
lengths of tree trunk and fixed to the wall.
Here are some examples.

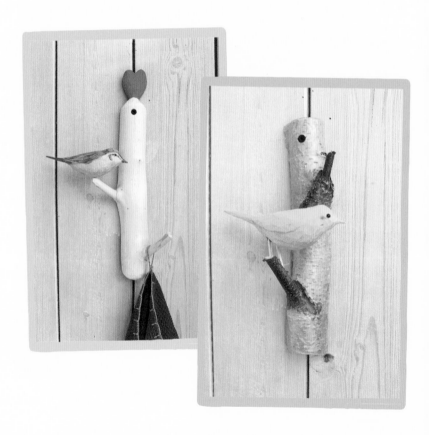

GROUPS OF BIRDS

For a bigger display, you can group your carved birds in pleasing compositions around branches or other forest finds. Here are some beautiful examples.

BIRDHOUSE

To make a cute birdhouse for your bird to live
in, choose a solid piece of wood of around
5 × 10 × 25cm (2 × 4 × 10in) and make a simple box,
sawn at an angle to accommodate the roof. Drill
an entrance hole in the front of the box, approx.
20–25mm (⅘in) in diameter. You can use strips
of wood, twigs, bark or other material to make the
roof. Paint the outside of the bird box and paint
inside the hole in black, then paint the roof and
nail or glue it in position.

Carve the baby bird as shown in the diagram so
that it fits into the hole, and glue in place or screw
in place from behind. Choose a twig to be used as
a perch, drill a hole in the nesting box and glue it
in position. Attach a picture hook to the back of
the box so it can be hung on a wall, and mount the
bird on the perch (see page 72).

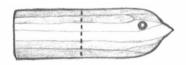

MORE ADVANCED BIRD PROJECTS

● ● ● ● ● ● ● ● ●

Once you've mastered whittling and mounting birds, you can go on to make all sorts of exciting projects, both decorative and practical. Here are some ideas.

BIRD MOBILE

A group of birds can be hung from a ring of
plaited willow or birch twigs, or can be suspended
one beneath the other, separated by pine cones,
beads or other decorative material. To suspend
a bird on a length of string, drill a hole in the
top of the bird 2.5–3mm ($\frac{1}{10}$–$\frac{1}{8}$in) in diameter,
then insert the string and glue it into the hole,
squeezing a matchstick down into the hole as a
wedge and breaking off the end of the match.

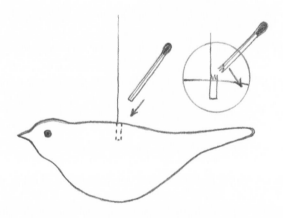

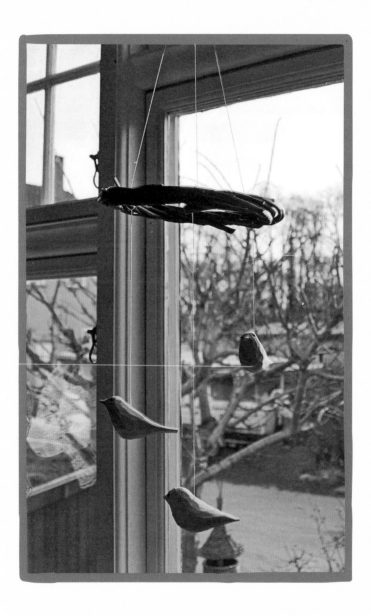

PECKING BIRDS

MATERIALS

2 strips of wood of 8 × 20mm (⅓ × ⅘in), length approx. 40cm (16in)

Small nails, length 20mm (⅘in)

2 pieces of dowel, 8mm (⅓in) in diameter, length approx. 8cm (3¼in)

Leather thong or similar material for the worm,
length approx. 15cm (6in), width approx. 2mm (1/12in)

1. Drill holes in the underside of the birds and insert the pieces of dowel. Glue the dowel in if you wish.

2. Drill holes in the beaks for the worm.

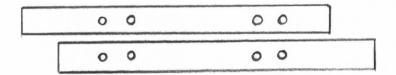

diagram 1

3. Make two rectangular holes in each strip of wood, spaced far enough apart to allow room for the birds and the worm. The holes in the two strips should be the same distance apart (see diagram 1).

4. Drill 8mm (⅓in) holes and remove the wood in between as in diagram 2 (see page 102).

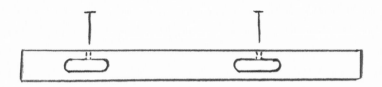

diagram 2

5. Drill a small hole 1.5–2mm ($\frac{1}{16}$–$\frac{1}{12}$in) in diameter from the side into the rectangular holes (see diagram 2).

6. Mount the birds on the upper strip first. Decide how high up you want them to sit and drill holes in the dowels (see diagram 3).

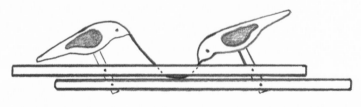

diagram 3

7. Insert the nails so you can see where the beaks hit the strip and drill holes for the worm at those points (see diagram 4).

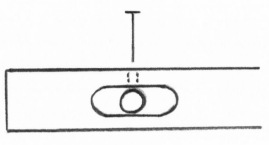

diagram 4

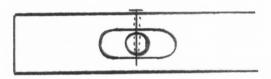

diagram 5

8. Nail the dowels in place (see diagram 5).

9. Glue the worm into the beak of one of the birds, thread through the strip of wood, adjust the length and glue the other end into the other bird's beak.

10. Assemble the lower strip in the same way as the upper. NB There must be enough space between the two strips so they can move to and fro and ensure there is room in between them for the worm.

OTHER IDEAS

Carved birds can add a decorative touch to
many practical items, from a kitchen roll holder
to a wine bottle stopper. The only limit is
your imagination!

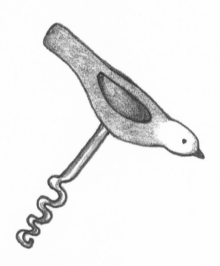

DRUMMING WOODPECKER

When the string is pulled, the woodpecker pivots and drums on the piece of tree. It also makes a good door knocker as the door will amplify the sound!

1. Carve the body of a woodpecker and its beak separately.

2. Drill a hole in the bird's head and glue the beak in position (see page 35).

3. Drill a hole 8mm (⅓in) in diameter in the woodpecker's breast and insert a dowel.

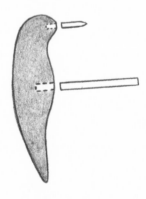

4. Drill three holes 8mm (⅓ in) in diameter in a piece of tree trunk cut in half. Remove the wood in between with a chisel or a knife to make a rectangular hole all the way through.

5. At the back of the trunk, gouge out a channel downwards from the rectangular hole to prevent the string from jamming.

6. Drill a hole 2mm (¹⁄₁₂ in) in diameter through the piece of trunk from the side.

7. Insert the woodpecker's dowel into the rectangular hole to determine how close to the trunk it should be positioned in order to rock backwards and forwards and strike the trunk with its beak, then mark with a nail where to drill the hole in the dowel.

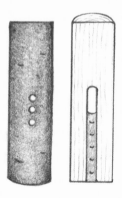

8. Fasten the woodpecker loosely in place with the nail. Mark and saw off the excess dowel.

9. Drill a hole through the end of the dowel and tie a string through it.

10. Put the woodpecker in place, insert the nail, and test to see if it works before hammering the nail in firmly.

11. Tie a bead or a twig to the end of the string for easy pulling.

12. Drill a hole in the top of the piece of trunk and screw the woodpecker door knocker in place.

POP-UP BIRD

When the string is pulled, the bird peeps
out of the hole.

1. Drill a hole 25-30mm (1-1¼in) in diameter through a piece of dry branch, approx. 50mm (2in) thick and 11-13cm (4⅖-5¼in) long. You're basically drilling out the inside of the branch.

2. Drill a peephole at the top of the branch for the bird to peep through.

3. Drill a hole approx. 5mm (⅕in) in diameter for the string, roughly halfway between the peephole and the bottom edge.

4. Carve a bird that fills the hole but can easily slide up and down. The bird's length should be adapted so that it is out of sight when it is down.

5. If you like, paint the bird's head and give it eyes.

6. Cut a notch in the bottom of the bird and drill a hole approx. 2.5mm (⅒in) in diameter (see diagram).

 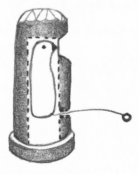

7. Glue a piece of string into the hole. Squeeze a matchstick with glue on it into the hole and break off the excess. The piece of matchstick acts as a wedge.

8. Insert the bird in the hollowed-out branch and thread the string from the inside out through the string hole. If necessary, fish the string out by inserting a piece of thin wire with a hooked end in through the hole.

9. Test to see if it works and adjust if necessary.

10. Tie a bead to the end of the string.

11. Cut a suitably sized disc from a branch to use as a base and glue or screw into position.

USEFUL
INFORMATION

TEMPLATES

These templates can also be used for birds other
than those indicated. Use a wood thickness of
3.5–4.5cm (1²⁄₅–1⁴⁄₅in) for these birds.

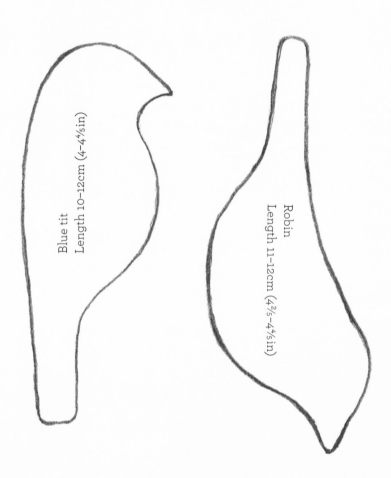

Blue tit
Length 10–12cm (4–4⁴⁄₅in)

Robin
Length 11–12cm (4²⁄₅–4⁴⁄₅in)

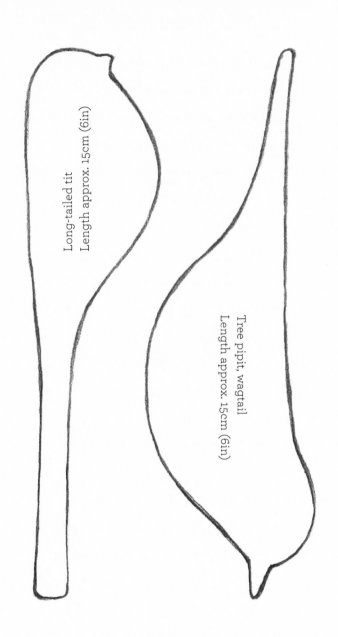

Long-tailed tit
Length approx. 15cm (6in)

Tree pipit, wagtail
Length approx. 15cm (6in)

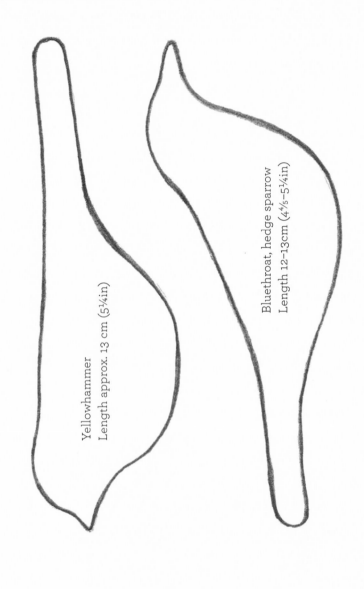

Yellowhammer
Length approx. 13 cm (5¼in)

Bluethroat, hedge sparrow
Length 12–13cm (4⅘–5¼in)

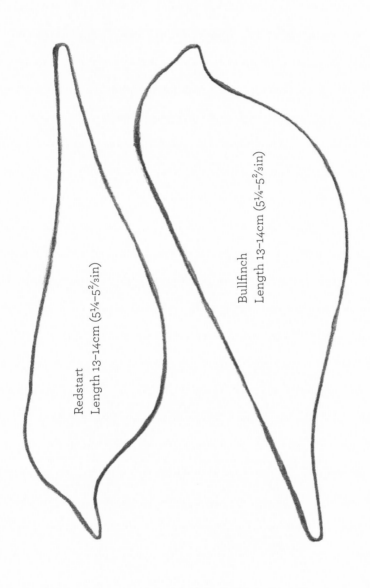

Redstart
Length 13-14cm (5¼-5²/₃in)

Bullfinch
Length 13-14cm (5¼-5²/₃in)

WHITTLING BOARD

Using a whittling board helps support and protect your whittling project as you work. Here's how to make your own.

1. Draw the shape of the board on the plywood and cut it out.

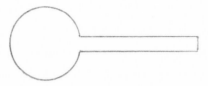

MATERIALS

Plywood, minimum thickness 15mm (²⁄₃in), width 25–30cm (10–12in), length 65–75cm (25–30in) For children, cut it a bit shorter.

Piece of wood for the front, suggested thickness 3cm (1¼in), approx. 5 × 10cm (2 × 4in).

2. Saw a notch in the piece of wood (see diagram and photograph).

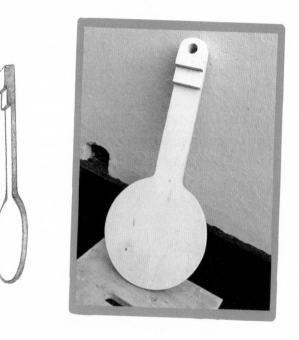

3. Glue the piece of wood in place or attach with screws on the underside. If you like, drill a hole in the end, wide enough to take the sheath of your knife while you are whittling, and for hanging the board up afterwards.

SUPPLIERS

Author's website and Etsy shop
www.snittesiden.dk
www.etsy.com/shop/Whittlingsale

• • • • •

Wood and whittling tools suppliers

UK
Isca Woodcrafts www.iscawoodcrafts.co.uk
G&S Specialist Timber www.toolsandtimber.co.uk
Classic Hand Tools www.classichandtools.com
The Toolpost www.toolpost.co.uk
Ockenden Timber www.ockenden-timber.co.uk

USA
Smoky Mountain Woodcarvers www.woodcarvers.com
Traditional Woodworker www.traditionalwoodworker.com
Wood Carvers Supply www.woodcarverssupply.com
Treeline www.treelineusa.com

• • • • •

Whittling and carving organisations and other bird whittlers
British Woodcarvers' Association
www.britishwoodcarversassociation.com
The Bird Whittler www.thebirdwhittler.co.uk
Nick's Birds www.nicksbirds.com
Nicke Helldorff www.handochtanke.se
Tom Nilsson www.tomtrasnidare.com
Vesa Jussila www.naturdiorama.se

ACKNOWLEDGEMENTS

With thanks to my dear wife Lillian, who did the
illustrations, took photos and helped with the
layout of the original Danish book.

ABOUT THE AUTHOR

Frank Egholm is the father of five
boys and has taught for 20 years at
a school in Denmark; teaching has
also been a source of inspiration for
the many ideas in his craft books.
He is the founder of Denmark's
annual whittling festival.

Denmark's
first whittling
festival in 2015.
Handicraft,
enjoyment and
good company.

INDEX